I0151436

Set the Table

poems by

Nina Clements

Finishing Line Press
Georgetown, Kentucky

Set the Table

ACKNOWLEDGMENTS

The following poems appeared in *Anderbo.com*:

Corner Table
Come for Dinner
Independent Kitchen
We Count Together

Publisher: Leah Maines

Editor: Christen Kincaid

Cover Art: Joshua Finnell

Author Photo: Jennifer M. Zosh

Cover Design: Elizabeth Maines McCleavy

Printed in the USA on acid-free paper.
Order online: www.finishinglinepress.com
             also available on amazon.com

Author inquiries and mail orders:
Finishing Line Press
P. O. Box 1626
Georgetown, Kentucky 40324
U. S. A.

Table of Contents

For my family

The Kitchen

When it's all used up
between us, there will still
be a kitchen: a cracked

floor to sweep, chipped
plates to scrape, and one
perfect red table. But now

there is only the high-pitched
whistle, louder than cicadas,
higher than live wire, that

fine chord of silence.

The Seven-House Man

In his seventh house,
the man rests easily
and eats nothing

but sesame seeds. He fries
them and sucks the oil
as he swallows, spitting

out the occasional burned
seed, the hard kernel
with which he can do nothing.

They gather at his feet,
the black specks. Someone
will sweep them away

as he sleeps.
It is the least sordid
of all his houses.

Corner Table

"Do you like mint tea?" when asked
in a quiet voice, in the dark
corner of a restaurant,

means really: *Do you*
like me? And when she
answers, "I care

passionately for olives,"
she means, of course,
You are a definite possibility.

Untitled

It's some June evening—
your mother is dying.
And we, my friend, are

not well either.
It's all balled up within us,
and yet we grip each other

with such fierceness.
I can no longer make a fist—
my palms have gone slack

from the effort.
There is no air, only the hum
of mowing lawns, the fan

in the next room. Electricity
is everywhere, but nothing
moves. Our mothers

are disappearing this year.
Will they take us
with them?

Independent Kitchen

Is it better, now, to slice
the cilantro alone—a silver
blade along the leaf's vein
separating one side from another?

When was it that we were
a team with a cutting board
in my kitchen—the smell
of garlic on our sticky,
sticky fingers?

A Note of Gratitude

Dear mother, in all my honesty,
you ruin everything. But I do thank
you, nonetheless, for your gift

of stoneware. An entire set! My
word, how generous. And yet,
we, by which I mean I, cannot

accept. Can you imagine—your solemn
face, your scowl and furrowed brow
with each forkful of butter beans?

In each slurp of soup, the gray taste
of stone? I do not live in Charlotte Brontë novels!
Please make a note of it. I will

not break my teeth upon the stone
each day—your stony eyes
and hollowed-out anger.

Every gift from you is a burden
in disguise. I am not the one
you wanted, but it is too late

for all that. And so, it is with sincerity
that I send this stack of stone
back to you. We will not break together.

Come for Dinner

After you have scraped
every good thing
from the pan,

let us sit down.
Let us talk. Eat
with your fingers.

Let them drip tomato
seeds before me. Listen.
Give me your heart

to hold while you chew.
I will want to keep it
because of its odd girth,

the satisfying solidity
of it against my palm.
But you and I

are for dinner only:
you will eat; we will talk;
and I will give the heart back.

Pantoum

In the center of her unrest
is one square of red, a table
of painted-over pine. The rest
is a blur she sees when she is able.

Only one square of red, a table
near the door. He stands beside her,
a blur she sees when she is able.
He is going; he is going. Does she prefer

this? Near the door, he stands beside her—
hard heart wrapped in bone, wrapped in skin.
He is going; he is going, and yet they demur.
What is it that makes the air so thin?

The hard heart is wrapped in bone, wrapped in skin
and in painted-over pine. The rest
is going, going. It cannot be deferred,
her unrest, the center of her distress.

Villanelle

Something of your life will return to you,
even in the fall: a tear of green leaf
in the center of your perfect palm. Do

anything you like. Drag your feet in dew;
get as muddy as you can. Hold your grief.
Something of your life will return to you

over mountains, through rivers. Breathe the few
gasps of wheat in the breeze. You held the sheaf
in the center of your perfect palm. Do

something for yourself this fall. Grow a new
mother from the black walnuts you can reach.
Something of your life will return to you:

the soft green leaf, the old oak tree. You grew
tomatoes, vines bound to stakes: each to each.
In the center of your perfect palm—do

you remember—were fireflies, bright. The cue
to go, quiet now, inside. What relief.
Something of your life will return to you
in the center of your perfect palm. Do.

An Early Eulogy

Take up your heart in your swollen hands, old man,
and give it another squeeze. You turn purple, gray,
purple gray: an old sausage within its skin.
Who will carry your coffin when it all gives way?

Your blood, the last blood of your sad, dead
family, cannot be thicker than water.
Where are your children? You demand them,
command them, in breathy gasps, to love you:

your weak heart, the girth of your failed body.
When it's time, they'll see you in your box—
double-wide, special-ordered, a monument
to all your effort, too heavy for the hearse.

For Every Thing You Add, You Are One Less

With each green seam sucked into the machine,
you are less. Oh, the long thread of mucus,
how it never ends, only grows thin, mean.
Is it deformity? Decay, no fuss,
only more beeps and screens, more skin to slough?
You are less, and yet the shadow cast is
olive trees in sun, though the bark is rough.
Did you want me, will you haunt me, fingers
pointed, concentric circles of age for
skin? You are less but more expanisve
in my imagination's cavern: Flor?
Each flower you painted, each leaf, pensive;
each thought, expensive. Wear your garland now,
while moss, that once was skin, softens your brow.

Lovers

"It takes so much to keep you
pleased," he tells me, but he means,
It takes so much to keep you

quiet. Is speech only chatter
then, a wash of white noise to be
ignored? I hate that I must talk

incessantly of the price of plums,
of a groundhog's evidence. Yet,
there are silences enough: a thumb

pressed upon the lower lip, a splay
of fingers across the neck.
His pleasure inside such moments.

Reconciled Movements

My mother told the doctor:
"It looks like I'm beating her,
but I haven't had any

of the fun of *doing* it."
She laughed loud, raspy,
shifting the weight of her

body from left to right foot,
smoothly combed hair bouncing
in time with her movement. I

remember: I sat on white
paper that crinkled beneath
me. He stared through the thickness

of glasses at the outline
of my leg, illuminated
by pink and purple splotches.

"I bruise easily," I said,
shy with the telling of it,
feeling what it really means

to sit: to feel the body's
whole weight concentrated
in one aggravated space.

I wanted there to be some
thing technically wrong
with me, something to tell

people when they asked what I
had done to myself. I became
a cut-out doll, the lines

of my joints dotted with bruises.
When I was three, I couldn't
stop bumping into walls. They

didn't do anything wrong,
so both parents took me
in the car, sun on my face,

to the city hospital.
It was nothing
serious, only "delayed

motor skills," yet both younger
sisters moved freely. My skin
touched the plastered coolness

of our walls every day.
What is the matter with us
that we must have everything

vertical and aligned, so
reverent to gravity?
You will never make me perfect.

Private Lake

Love is white skin stretched
swollen, like I've been beaten,
surfacing like dead fish in a lake,
broken ridges of reds and purples.

This is what love is, I tell myself,
fog hovering around me,
around purple water, the lake
a liquid bruise in moonlight.

Love is a succession of finger-bruises
up my arms, his skin pressing, thumbs
against my fleshy undersides. I like love,
I tell myself. Like being marked,

tracing the line from hand to heart of
dotted blue bumps, as though I'd been
stitched back together with bruises,
scarred, and for a moment, I long

for sloppy-tongue kisses,
saliva sticking on my bare, fresh leg
that dissolves now, in muddled water,
along the seams of my cutout doll self,

like I was his paper-cut voodoo doll,
wondering what he thinks about when he
touches me, callused thumbs on pressure
points, marks turning yellow in his absence.

Almost a Pantoum: An Anniversary Evening

You brush my bare arm with a callous hand
and trace its shadow down my body in your bed.
Lying on my back, I see bruises in the spots
of my eyes, purpling the bare ceiling.

I trace my fingers down your body
as though a touchstone and test with my tongue.
My eyes close against the spots of purple
that mark your body with eggplant stains.

I taste the eggplant with my tongue, wishing
it were cool Autumn again, feet touching
with pure interest. Your aloe plant rots
in the corner, peeling away from the sun.

In this hot Autumn, feet, arms, bodies fall;
lying on my back, I can reach your bruises
with my fingers, though you peel away.
I brush your bare arm with a callused hand.

Saying Good-Bye

I buried your face
in our old desperate
place, against

the bark and vine leaves.
It used to be
our sanctuary—

embalmed dragonflies
in spider webs,
tiny capsuled coffins.

I learned to steal those
sticky-coated pearls
and swallow them whole,

my face, soft, touching
bark, ants crawling
across my forehead.

They gathered square
granules of salt
from my hair,

nourishing
and sticky
in the oil.

What We Find Missing

Somebody robbed my eighty-year-old
grandmother, broke into her narrow house,
jagged with age and wear, in the middle

of the week. She lives there alone
with two birds, a hip replacement,
and a leaky knee. When my mother

told me this, her voice scratched
with connection. In small moments,
I saw Grandmother enshrined in her

living room, her white sweatshirt shimmery
with gold necklaces, her pink sweatpants with one leg
rolled up, to show the swelling to anyone who asks.

Who could imagine someone would scale
the slants of her crooked house?
Who could imagine someone wanted her old

sweaters, her grandmotherly gold jewelry
so badly? "They have no respect,"
she says afterward. "They just want the money

for the drugs." Her voice is thick
with accent, with pain, and with assurance.
"Nothing can kill this woman,"
my mother told me long-distance, relieved.

"She was always lucky." No one forgets this.
She's finding things missing: an Italian sweater,
a photograph of my grandfather

in a good frame, orange prescription bottles
full of his old teeth. My mother
used to find crumpled-up Kleenex

in the linen closet after Grandmother
left, pressed between sheets and towels.
"Every time she came back,

she would check
to make sure
they were gone."

Truck Stop Frailty

I.

My mother told me never to go
out—to leave—past midnight
but to stay, just beneath the coverlet, ready.

Instead, I spend those nights at the truck stop
beneath its vaulted rafters. Wood
angles and touches to form a perfect point above—

a country church, arched, meeting high
above our heads.
A window in the loft slides the darkness in.

II.

Flush against the corner
walls, anatomized
and separate, we form

the connections, the background,
of empty space.
There is

a secular holiness
in this sharing
of place. Without distinction

there is a separate pluralism:
truckers shower,
students read and underline,

and waitresses serve the food
on chipped
and dirty dishes, all undisturbed.

With David, en route to the SanVito Funeral Home to View the Body of a Sixteen-Year-Old Eagle Scout

The last thing I ever told my grandfather
was the Dinner Prayer. I answered the phone:
"Bless us O Lord, and these, thy gifts."

Prayer through the hospital connection:
"Which we are about to receive, through thy bounty
through Christ, our Lord. Amen."

I didn't realize what I had done, that language
had left me behind until he asked to speak
to my father, to tell him something final,

I thought years later. Afterward, I imagined hearing
the quick intake of his breath, unsteady
and surprised as I flung the phone away,

instrument of my guilt. My parents found
me hours later, in a makeshift confessional
between window and curtain,

silent and scourged with a finger
up my nose. You laugh at me,
but I was only seven, and they never

told me he was dying. That was the last
thing I ever said to him.
I know this is not the same,

but we can never surpass the guilt
we feel coupled with the loss.
We will always be deceived in the timing of it.

Almost a Pantoum: Midnight Sky

Loose fingers of pink and purple slide
together across the dull, dark sky.
We sit silently watching the emptiness,
my head tucked against your hard shoulder.

We sit together, dull against the darkness,
feeding blank eyes toward the oscillating
clouds that contract, separate,
giving us a glimpse of stars in the cold.

We feed our eyes across the sky, separate
from each other, pressed into stone
but still touching. How is it that we
can imagine a heartbeat, feel it without sound?

Close to each other, pressed into one another
against the cold, we sit silently, watching
for signs, feeling the air change
as loose fingers slide across the sky.

Birth

First there was the rupture:
the crack of the egg, a slice
of pain. There is always

this rupture—this bursting
and cleaving of split sides
as I have burst and cleaved

from you. It is an opening
and closing of the jewel
case, but the first crack

is irrevocable, a fine
thread of pain—circling,
circling—until it has

got round me so
completely, and then *I*
am the egg, and then *I*

am the fine thread
of pain—or worse,
the jewel case.

It is a dream;
it is not a dream.
It is my body, speaking.

Dreaming Dora

I see her sitting
quite stiffly on his
opulent Turkish couch,

tasseled and pillowed
about. But I cannot tell
what she wore, what she

wanted there. It could not
have been him, the gray
doctor and his glasses,

his white hair—perhaps
a cigar between his teeth,
in front of her, even.

Eighteen and stiff-backed,
opening, closing, opening
closing that small

reticule. I see her sitting
in stillness, silent,
just the sound of clicking,

a wordless rhythm:
open, shut, open
shut. I see her sitting.

In my dream, of course,
I ask her, Who did you
love, Dora? Who did you

want? Who really gave
you that pretty little catarrh,
that pretty little cough,

so delicate in its scratchiness,
so resistant to Freud's attack?

We Count Together

I.

"How many breaths do you
have left?" I ask her.
We are dreaming, so

the question is not really
that strange. When she doesn't
answer, I persist: "Are there

a lot? Too many to count?"
Her face is smooth again
with the wisdom of a deity.

In her illness, as in my dreams,
she knows something more
than I do. For the first time,

I do not understand, can
no longer read, the arch
of her eyebrows, the turn

of her lips, but I know
my sister feels this loneliness
as real as I feel the swish

of her hair, the whip of her
neck as she turns, turns, turns
against me, upon waking.

II.

Once, a long time ago,
I counted breaths out
loud, holding my ear

to your heart. Dreaming,
I can remember this,
your babyness, the black

scab of your belly like
a jewel to me. But
dreaming blends time,

and suddenly you have
become a cat, our lovely
cat, who was dying

when I held him at the last.
I counted for him:
in, out, in out.

Sonnet

The dream remains the same: her father stands
in the bathtub, enclosed by yellow tiles.
He has died, suddenly, but is stranded
there, near the toilet, where she sits and smiles.
Finally, they are alone. When he speaks,
it's a whisper, softer than the faucet
that trickles its slight stream, hardly a leak,
down to the marble sink. She had wanted
it so much, as a girl, this privacy.
No matter her waking age, in the dream
she wears her first communion's dress. Brightly,
her voice echoes off the tiles. His eyes gleam,
yellow lights in the dark brown. Now she hates
this dream. She wakes, mouth twisted in distaste.

Unfinished

There is nothing left of my
two closed lips. My mouth
couldn't be more chapped and
wide. I will confess away
to any man for a smile
and a silver coin—the kind
that grants passage on
the merry-go-round, the dirty
one in our formerly dirty little
town. When he was a child,
my father would not share his coin
but kept it in his thin, dusty hand.

Any open-air confessional will do—
a park bench with grooved, wooden slats,
the pigeons and their dirty droppings.
I'll sit down upon it and tell you:
everything. And I will do it with a wistful
smile. And I will do it for free—you can
forget your silver coin.

Reign of Ants

No matter how hard I look, one turns up,
floating in my tea, triumphant
and dead. I had inspected everything so
carefully—the spoon, the cup, the tea itself
(reheated to avoid waste). I had
stirred it in with the cream, suddenly
there in a tide of tannins.
The cream is gone, so I scooped it out
into the sink to join its sisters, but
they will no doubt rise again. And who
am I to be so significant, to insist
that insects will not march up and down
the length of me until I'm gone, until
it won't matter? The cosmic importance
of the self—it never ends.

Dreaming Ants

In the dream, there is an itch,
slow, subtle, then a stitch in the
abdomen. There is the fear of
giving birth, of breathing out
a mess between one's legs. All that
blood and being, and it will
squeal and squawk and be a bother,
quite possibly grow up to hate you.
How can people bear the
responsibility, the longevity,
of such love?
In the dream, the itch is twisted and
dark. I am afraid.
But when I wake, there are only ants,
marching single file across my belly.

Nina Clements attended Denison University before earning an MFA in creative writing from Sarah Lawrence College. She now works as a librarian in Southern California. *Set the Table* is her first collection.

www.ingramcontent.com/pod-product-compliance
Lightning Source LLC
LaVergne TN
LVHW051612080426

835510LV00020B/3256